Okinum

Okinum

Émilie Monnet

SCIROCCO DRAMA

Okinum
first published 2022 by Scirocco Drama
An imprint of J. Gordon Shillingford Publishing Inc.
© 2022 Émilie Monnet

Scirocco Drama Editor: Glenda MacFarlane

Cover artwork by Meky Ottawa
Cover design by Doowah Design
Photo of Émilie Monnet by Christian Blais

Printed and bound in Canada on 100% post-consumer recycled paper.
We acknowledge the financial support of the Manitoba Arts Council and
The Canada Council for the Arts for our publishing program.

Production inquiries to:
Valérie Cusson
Cusson Management
1760 des Abbesses,
Saint-Jérôme, QC
J7Z 0E7, Canada
Office: 450.990.1214
Mobile: 514.892.5399
valerie@cussonmanagement.com

Library and Archives Canada Cataloguing in Publication

Title: Okinum / Émilie Monnet.
Other titles: Okinum. English
Names: Monnet, Émilie, 1978- author.
Description: A play. | Translation of: Okinum.
Identifiers: Canadiana (print) 20220196532 | Canadiana (ebook) 20220212449 |
ISBN 9781927922934 (softcover) | ISBN 9781990737121 (HTML)
Classification: LCC PS8626.O547 O4513 2022 | DDC C842/.6—dc23

J. Gordon Shillingford Publishing
P.O. Box 86, RPO Corydon Avenue, Winnipeg, MB Canada R3M 3S3

Kitci Meegwetc Kokom Mani
eki pejjinjawotc Amik
kidja weshbamek
Mii e aji
E wejibamagwa
Ni Moshommik
Oken dananawa
Kishpen kendamik tebi o odjibawik.

Émilie Monnet

At the intersection of theatre, performance and sound, Émilie Monnet's practice is centred on themes of memory and transformation and is often produced through a collaborative process. The artistic processes rely on an approach characterized by being present, listening, caring for what surrounds us, and nurturing relationships with the human and natural worlds. As a writer, performer, and director, Monnet's work takes the form of interdisciplinary theatre, performance installations and immersive sound experiences. Monnet is both Algonquin and French and grew up in the Outaouais, Quebec and Brittany, France. *Okinum* is her first written play.

Playwright's Note

I have always been fascinated by dreams

when waking up
I've even got into the habit of staying in that state between
sleeping and waking
where it's easier to hold on to dreams
just before they slip away
and disappear
way inside my psyche

what I remember
are fragments
strange cinematographic situations
that leave me with vivid images
or words
whispered in my ear
while sleeping
whose meaning I try to decipher later

I have a notebook
where I like to write down my dreams
to make sure I remember them
I keep them alive
by retelling them
and paying attention to them
they open new portals
pathways into my imagination
into the deep pockets of my memory

It's because of my dream of Micha Amik that I learnt that giant
beavers once existed.
Their recurrent visit in my sleep was the impulse to paddle up
my inner river to better understand where I come from.
Amik became my guide in this poetic journey of building and
removing a dam in my throat.
And for Amik's teachings, I will always be grateful.

Foreword
Emma Tibaldo

Okinum is built on layers of knowledge.

It began as a series of monologues inspired by Émilie's dreams of the beaver, Amik.

It has grown into a sharing of experience, and ancestral knowledge. It is a stunning journey through fear to finding strength and inner courage, and ultimately leads to Émilie speaking her truth.

It is a story of growth, and progression-reconnection to ancient knowing, and the struggle of contemporary existence.

It is a manifesto to resilience. It is a call to arms. It is strong and unapologetic. It is Émilie at her most vulnerable, and therefore her fiercest.

This work of art, this sharing of experience, this journey to reclamation found its full voice, in large part, because Émilie fought so very hard to find the space, time, collaborators, and resources equal to the breath of her creative exploration. This publication is a culmination of the discoveries made through the many residencies secured during its development.

Émilie created *Okinum* through a rigorous circular process of researching, writing, rehearsing, performing, back to researching, rewriting, rehearsing, performing. Each stage of performance inviting Émilie to reach further into her truth, removing all that felt untrue or not connected to her understanding of her history. As she continues to reclaim, and absorb, so too does the play. It has evolved and changed with every new production. It is in constant evolution—a living history that grows and becomes sharper, clearer, with every performance.

Each iteration of the play's production history was supported by research and creation residencies. This allowed the creative team to experiment with sound, lights, and video throughout the creative stages of building and defining the elements needed to tell this story. My first encounter with this development process was as co-director. The company went up to the University of Quebec in Chicoutimi to participate as part of an offering by the Research Chair in Creation for Sound Dramaturgy in Theatre. An incredible amount of experimentation in story structure, and in sound design happened during this week. What emerged was the blueprint for the performance of the play. The link between Émilie, and sound designer, composer, and performer Jackie Gallant was firmly established, and remains a defining aspect of the production.

This was followed by further residencies, where we all worked to integrate the essential storytelling elements of video and lighting into the building of the play's universe. We discovered the specificity of the story's movement through time, the non-linear, yet forward moving energy of the piece. We established a process where every aspect of the theatrical world was being developed, simultaneously.

The creative team was invited to bring all of themselves to the process. As a co-director and dramaturg, my focus at this stage was supporting Émilie in her quest to finding meaningful images she could explore on stage as an actor, and to rediscover how she built her play so that the depth of the journey could be communicated to an audience. Émilie, Jackie, my co-director Sarah, and I worked hard to remove any sense of hierarchy in the rehearsal room, finding the most genuine way of bringing Émilie's world to life on stage. Émilie was clear from the very beginning that the play would happen in the round. And so we worked in the round. Story development, movement, staging, visual and aural elements, all working together, in a circular pattern, much like the space itself. We listened to each other, built on each other's ideas, and proposals, without edges, always folding ideas into the work: Round and round, deeper and deeper. Émilie wanted the audience to sit inside the story. She wanted them to experience the play as if they were in the belly of a beaver lodge with her.

I believe the sense of being immersed inside this dreamscape world was achieved. Visuals were projected on five screens placed on the outermost perimeter of the audience seating, with Émilie on a pentagonal shaped structure in the center. This meant that no matter where the audience was seated in the round, they experienced Émilie's performance surrounded by the evocative visuals. Sound designer, composer, and performer Jackie Gallant was placed in the audience. She had a direct connection to Émilie's performance, allowing for an instinctual live conversation between the two performers. The soundscape, much like the visual world, surrounded the audience, creating the sense of being enveloped, cocooned inside the world of the play.

Following the premiere, and subsequent publication of *Okinum* in French, Émilie embarked on the next phase in the development of this story, the translation, and adaption of *Okinum* into English. In so doing, she had to reconsider which experiences in the story belonged to which of the three languages that lived inside of her. Ultimately, this process gave Émilie the time and space to expand the parts of the story that cried out to be expressed in Anishnaabemowin—the language of her grandfather, and of her great-great-grandmother Mani. Émilie used this opportunity to rediscover her own creation, delve further into the images, and explore the language's impact on her journey.

It was during the intensive period of mounting the production in English, that Émilie discovered the need to reimagine the ending for the play. Her understanding of her own journey through illness and recovery had crystallized, and through this she understood that the story's pivotal discovery belonged to her ancestral language. And so, as part of the structure of the play, the final Amik encounter is revealed in Anishnaabemowin. This new ending is a reflection of her true journey to discovery, connection, and voice.

Okinum is a fierce example of how a story, a creation, a truth, can continue to evolve and change past the first production, past its original publication, and light the way to a richer, fuller, path to storytelling, and authenticity in theatre. Listening to your intuition and folding in new discoveries are superhuman strengths. Émilie has shared her strengths with us through this work.

January 2022

Emma Tibaldo is a director and dramaturg-collaborating with many playwrights across the country. She is also a budding drummer.

Production History

The English version of *Okinum* premiered in September of 2021 as part of Centaur Theatre's Brave New Looks program, produced by Onishka Productions and Imago Theatre, in collaboration with Playwrights' Workshop Montréal.

Writer, Translator, Co-Director, and Performer:	Émilie Monnet
Co-Directors:	Emma Tibaldo Sarah Williams
Sound Designer and Performer:	Jackie Gallant
Voice Performers:	Véronique Thusky, Thérèse Thelesh Bégin
Stage Manager:	Luciana Burcheri
Set Designer:	Simon Guilbault
Lighting Designer:	Lucie Bazzo
Costume Designer:	Caroline Monnet
Moccasins:	Sage Paul
Video Designer:	Clark Ferguson
Dramaturgs:	Emma Tibaldo Sarah Williams
Anishnaabemowin Language and Culture Consultant:	Véronique Thusky
Translation Dramaturg:	Maureen Labonté
Sound and Technical Director:	Frédéric Auger
Sound Operator:	Simon Riverin

Okinum was first produced in French at Montreal's Centre du Théâtre d'Aujourd'hui in 2018.

Foreword
Véronique Thusky

Kawin onikeken kida anishnaabemowin
Mindjamenen ki sogodewin
Ka'n acitc kidjaskanaken sagiodewin
Mii dac ke mossekidamen kida ijitcigeiin
Kishpen nisistemin anishnaabemowin
Ningan wasek kiga ijionagon.

Language and knowledge keeper, Véronique Thusky is an Anishnaabe kwe from Barriere Lake, Quebec.

Photo by Andrée Lanthier.

There is a platform in the shape of a pentagon in the middle of the stage. It is covered with beaver pelts. Five copper video screens are suspended above the five sides of the pentagon. The pentagon is a magical shape. The lighting is warm and intimate. The space feels like an art installation. The audience is seated around the central platform.

SCENE 1: In Dream (Prologue)

Black. At first, we hear rumbling, then the sounds of frogs and beavers join in. A call-and-response starts between the beavers and a human voice. ÉMILIE appears from beneath the platform. This is her lodge. The blue light slowly reveals the magical shape of the pentagon where, in the middle, she is squatting. Then ÉMILIE speaks, addressing the spirits around her.

Nidaniamkowag
Ni moshomik mamowi ni kokomishimik
Miqwetc nidanak eki pakidanajiwodj kidji weshibadiman
Amik mashkikiwin kiguejiigewin atsokan iye
Apidendagozi aa Micha Amik kagi ijitigetch

The rumbling starts again. ÉMILIE begins to sing. Stars appear on the screens, sparse at first, then swirling and dancing. ÉMILIE stands up and raises her arms to catch the stars and swallows some. They are the ancestors up in the sky and hold the knowledge.

The rumbling intensifies. ÉMILIE is swallowed in a vortex of sound.

Photo by Andrée Lanthier.

SCENE 2: Small Game

> *ÉMILIE wakes up gasping for breath, as if from a dream that kept her tense all night long. She is sitting in the middle of the platform. Surrounded by white light.*

My heart beats fast
Intuition doesn't lie
Intuition
is my inner compass
A gift
Passed down from my mother
From her mother before her
A skill
to feel
from deep down
It's subtle
secret

> *We start hearing voices saying words in Anishinaabemowin. They're not really audible at first, more like whispers, caresses to the ear. As the scene progresses, the words become easier to understand.*

My great great-grandmother's name was Mani
I hear her voice
in my ears
buzzing
whispering
revealing
especially in my dreams
Dreams are premonitions
truths
visions
Dreams clear away the fog
from deep down
Words muttered
into my ear
to decipher dreams

Dreams that can also
sometimes
predict
death

That's the gift
No
Intuition
never
lies
In my bed
spread out
in the shape of a star
I listen
to my heart
 beating fast
too fast
since I left my dream
and landed here
awake

I have an appointment at the hospital this morning

Pause. We shift into Dream World.

I dreamt I was on the trap line
I dreamt of Wabush
caught in a snare.
I see Wabush struggle
for a long time
trying to break free
from the metallic fangs grasping at their neck
I watch
without moving
mesmerized
by rabbit's instinct to survive.

I look at Wabush
right in the eye
holding on to this moment
so fleeting

when life spills out
when fur becomes still

I'm transfixed

Right here
Right in front of me
I watch
Wabush
die

I admire their fight
Fur is white
as snow
Wabush finally surrender
Body stops shaking
Heart stops beating

Without a cry
or a plea
Wabush
offers
their life
in the crisp silence of winter.
I start to undress Wabush
remove their fur
The flesh is pink
warm
naked

I watch the blood
drip onto the snow
Nothing's more beautiful than this red spill
this blood-offering
now soaking into the white.

ÉMILIE stands up.

We hear a voice in Anishnaabemowin saying the following. ÉMILIE repeats some of the words.

Pakidadenagewin panema kida togon kijdja madiziwin.
Kek oshka madiziwin ki abidan.

Pause.

My heart beats faster
It means I'm alive
Right?
And since I found the lump
since I've entered this dance
with ultrasounds
mammograms
biopsies
scans
needles
under my skin
life
MY life
pulses
A dam about to break

I have an appointment at the hospital this morning
I feel like Wabush:
dépecée, exposée
dépecée, exposée
dépecée, exposed, raw
raw, vulnérable, skinned, vulnerable, dépecée
à vif, à vif, à vif

> *The rumbling starts again, and beaver sounds
> intensify. We tip into Beaver World.*

Photo by Andrée Lanthier.

SCENE 3: First Beaver Dream

> *Pre-recorded words in Anishnaabemowin interweave with live text, enveloping the audience in the sounds of language. Sounds of water. There is a river nearby.*
>
> *We shift into Dream World again.*

A beaver
Giant
Fur
So shiny

> *ÉMILIE recognizes Amik the beaver.*

Amik
Taller than me
Amik
Eyes lock
Walks towards me
Stands in front of me
Looks familiar
Amik
Grabs my hand
Puts something into my palm
A pouch
Amik says:
Owe ni mashkikim
Kin oo aji
Mino abijiton

> *Amik disappears.*

Amik?

> *She tries to remember Amik's message.*

Owe ni Mishki...

Now we hear a pre-recorded conversation between Émilie and Véronique Thusky, her Anishnaabemowin teacher. Émilie asks what the words spoken by the beaver in her dream meant. Véronique translates them into English. She also corrects Émilie's pronunciation. It's obvious she is learning the language. (Bold font indicates that ÉMILIE on stage says the same words as in the pre-recorded audio clip.)

Véronique: Owe ni mashkikim.

Émilie: **Owe ni mashkikim.**

Véronique: Owe ni mashkikim. This is my medicine.

Émilie: Then he said, Kin oo aji. (Pronounced incorrectly.)

Véronique: Kin oo aji   Kin oo aji.

Émilie: **Kin oo aji** (Repeating.)

Véronique: Hmum, this means it's yours now/

Émilie: /**Wow**

Véronique: because he gives it to you.

Émilie: And then he said, Mino abijiton. (Pronounced incorrectly.) **Something like that.**

Véronique: Mino abijiton.

Émilie: **Abijiton.**

Véronique: Mino abijiton. It means use it well. Abijiton means use it. Mino, it means carefully or well or even for the better. So, this is what it means, mino abijiton.

Émilie: Mino abijiton. Abijiton.

Véronique: Abijiton

Émilie: **Abijiton.**

End of recording.

Photo by Valérie Remise.

SCENE 4: A Dam in the Throat

> *We hear a National Geographic-style jingle. ÉMILIE steps down from the platform and speaks directly to the audience. Black-and-white documentary-style video footage of beavers in action.*

In July 1990, the same summer as the Oka / Kanesatake resistance and blockade, an enormous beaver dam was photographed by a NASA satellite. Nobody knew of its existence. Not until Google Earth...

The dam is right in the middle of Wood Buffalo National Park in Northern Alberta. It measures 850 meters, which is quite exceptional. Beaver dams rarely measure more than 10 meters.

Many generations of beaver worked on the construction of the dam and, to this day, the dam still continues to grow.

Where beavers build dams, new bodies of water appear, like deep stagnant ponds. These ponds also allow for new bacteria to develop in the water, breaking down pollutants caused by the overuse of chemical fertilizers.

It's remarkable how beavers restore life and how they repopulate their territories, after being hunted continuously, for hundreds of years.

Beavers are the only species along with humans able to leave a trace on Earth that is visible from outer space.

An imprint left on Earth.
A dam for protection.
But only visible from the stars.

> *She crawls back onto the platform, as if pulled in by what she sees projected in it. We hear a pre-recorded conversation between ÉMILIE and VÉRONIQUE.*

Émilie: *What does it mean "okinum"?*

Véronique: *Is a dam, beaver dam.*

Émilie: *Beaver dam.*

Véronique: *Beaver dam; "amik" is the beaver, "okinum" is the dam.*

Émilie: *And what's the root?*

Véronique: *Etymologically, it's "okin" means your bones, because the trees, they look like bones gathered together.*

So "okinum," it means like the corpse of the trees.

Okinum is: the skeletons that have been put together.

Well you could say almost as if all the corpses you put in a cemetery when they are gathered all together it's the bones of the trees.

Véronique: *"Okinum."*

Émilie: *"Okinum."*

Pause.

The woman repeats the word "Okinum." The "O" transforms into a sound in her throat, as if she is trying to unblock her throat.

Véronique: Menjesh Chapeney.

Émilie: Menjesh Chapeney?

Véronique: Menjesh Chapeney, Menjesh Chapeney.

Émilie: *And what does it mean?*

Véronique: *"Cancer."*

Émilie: *But what does it mean exactly?*

Véronique: *"Menjesh," the insects that give you disease or lack of health; "Chapeney" means lack of health that the Menjesh has done to you.*

Émilie: *So it is like, **insects eating you inside?***

Véronique: *The insects are like eating all your wellness.*

> *Superimposed images of an ultrasound of her throat and a giant beaver dam seen from the sky are projected on the screens. ÉMILIE touches her throat. Beaver sounds start, as if talking to ÉMILIE. She responds with sounds coming from her throat.*

Photo by Andrée Lanthier.

SCENE 5: A Little Something in the Throat

The invisible starts becoming visible.

She's in a hammock
The sky bursting with stars
All night she hears the taita sing
His voice
opening her soul
She sees everything in crazy colors
Red, yellow, green, purple, turquoise
interweaving and dancing
A multicolored snakeskin
A voice murmurs in her head:
"Open your mouth"

> *A pre-recorded voice is heard. ÉMILIE's mouth
> remains open for the rest of the scene.*

"Open your mouth wide"...

All night her mouth stays open
The yellow, red and orange
split the sky
and transform into a blade of light
penetrating her mouth
and piercing through her neck
C'est chaud là tout à coup

The voice in her head repeats:
"It will be okay"

> *End of pre-recorded voice. Back to live voice. She
> touches her throat.*

It will be okay
I will be okay

Photo by Andrée Lanthier.

SCENE 6: Fear

Deafening buzzing sounds. Flashing neon lights.

I'm here
in this waiting room
sitting here
in a blue hospital gown
waiting
a blue hospital gown in the middle of other blue gowns
people waiting
just like me
waiting to be called
to be told where to go
the number on the door of the room
to be told
finally
what to expect
I'm waiting
looking at the hands on the clock above the door
they're moving needles
going round and round endlessly
waiting
in waiting rooms
I have all the minutes in the world
to imagine the worst
to let fear take over
I'm scared of needles
I'm scared of this needle:
it's ten centimeters long
and they're going to plunge it
into my throat

I hate this blue hospital gown
I hate holding it shut behind my back
so you don't see my underwear
I hate feeling my skin
naked under the blue gown
more than anything
I hate being at the mercy of a needle

a needle ten centimeters long
piercing the hard lump
in my throat
sometimes it's so hard they have to push
scrape
play around with the needle
in my throat
I'm scared of this needle because it will determine what's next
lay me out
on this cold hospital table
make me feel trapped
caught in a snare
a snare of needles
piercing through the soft
skin
of my neck

There's a word In Anishnaabemowin for
the fear an animal feels when facing its predator:
Kaachikawazi
Kaachikawazi

> *The voices come back. This time, they are more*
> *audible.*

I'm scared
of the results of this new biopsy
of being tired
all the time
of not being able to work
of you
not kissing my neck
like before

I'm scared
I won't make the right decision
I'm scared this whole business about a gift
is all bullshit
bullshit stories we make up
to feel connected to something bigger
to an ancestor who had the gift

for healing
We all want extraordinary people in our family tree
Don't we?
I'm scared of the tick-tock of the clock
I'm scared of not leaving a trace
Kotaadjiwin: fear
Kotaanendâgoziwin: that which creates fear
Kotaadendagon: it's scary
Kotadji: to be afraid
Soongideye: to stop being afraid
Soongideye: to stop being afraid
Soongideye: to stop being afraid

> *ÉMILIE enters her magical circle. We tip into Dream World again.*

Photo by Andrée Lanthier.

SCENE 7: The Recurring Beaver Dream

> *Same beaver dream as the first one. This time in French.*

Amik vient encore me rendre visite
Je vois sa tête d'abord, à moitié sortie de l'eau
Puis ses dents
Orange
Presque fluo
Amik sort de l'eau
Plus grand que moi
Amik me prend la main
La retourne vers le ciel
Dans ma paume, un sac
Une peau

> *In Amik's voice.*

«Owe ni mashkikim.
Kin oo aji. Mino abijiton.»

> *ÉMILIE translates Amik's words in English, trying to make sense of them.*

This is my medicine
It's yours now
Make good use of it
But what IS your med...?
Amik?

> *With a piece of charcoal, ÉMILIE draws a big beaver on the birchbark while repeating the words in Anishnaabemowin from the recording.*

> *We hear the sounds of beavers biting into wood. Over top, a pre-recorded conversation between ÉMILIE and VÉRONIQUE.*

Émilie: If I want to ask Amik to help me, **how do I say it**?

Véronique: Widemoshin.

Émilie: *Widemoshin.*

Véronique: *Wiiiiiidemoshin.*

Émilie: **Wiiiiiidemoshin.**

Véronique: *Wiiiiiidemoshin.*

Émilie: **Wiiiiiidemoshin.**

Véronique: *E nabidek.*

Émilie: **E nabidek.**

Véronique: *E nabidek.*

Émilie: **E nabidek.**

Véronique: *Ni mashkikim.*

Widemoshin e nabidek ki mashkikim.

Émilie: **Widemoshin e nabidek ki mashkikim.**

Émilie: If I want to thank Amik for coming and visiting me in my dreams, **how would I say   that?**

Véronique: *Kidje weshbaminan.*

Émilie: **Kidje weshbaminan.**

Véronique: *Odji kiguewin kidje weshbaminan.*

Émilie: **Odji kiguewin.**

Véronique: *Kidje weshbaminaɲ hum….*

Émilie: **Kidje weshbaminan.**

Véronique: *Humhum... kidje weshbaminan.*

Émilie: **Kidje weshbaminan.**

Véronique: *Odji kiguewin kidje weshbaminan.*

Émilie: **What does it mean?**

Véronique: *To restore my health. This is why I dream of you…*

Véronique: *Thank you to visit me in my dreams and to allow me a path to healing.*

Émilie: *Hum…. **It's beautiful.***

Photo by Andrée Lanthier.

SCENE 8: Beaver's Teeth

*The National Geographic jingle starts. In a lecture-
style delivery, ÉMILIE removes the rest of the beaver
pelts, stacking them in a pile.*

From the 17th to the 19th century, beaver hats were one of the
most important features in a man's wardrobe in Europe. At the
time, it was a common belief that wearing a beaver hat would
make you smarter. And a deaf person could even recover their
hearing.

In Europe, beavers were almost extinct by the end of the
1700s. North America became a major supply source to
sustain fashion in Europe, and it's around that time that the
Hudson's Bay Company was created to export as many beaver
pelts as possible. Overhunted, beavers here almost vanished
completely by the end of the 1800s.

The beaver pelts were a form of currency in the development
of the colonial economy, which enabled Canada to come into
existence. It explains why the beaver became the official symbol
of Canadian sovereignty in 1975 and why it was chosen to be
on the nickel back in 1937. But in 2011, Senator Nicole Eaton
proposed a new law to replace the beaver on the coin with
a polar bear. The Senator considered the beaver to be a "has
been," no longer reflecting Canadian values.

"The beaver is a rat, a big rat. Every winter, they destroy the
docks at our cottages." The Senator's proposal was rejected,
and the beaver continues to be the iconic symbol of this country.

Amik needs to work all the time
because their teeth never stop growing
if Amik stops working
the teeth will pierce their throat.

*Beaver sounds transform into the sounds of birch-
bark biting, a traditional art form practised by
Indigenous women across Turtle Island.*

Photo by Andrée Lanthier.

SCENE 9: The Art of Making Marks on Bark

> *The image of a birchbark flower is projected on the platform.*

Mani is in a forest of birch trees
She cuts through the bark with her knife

A drop falls
Then another one
It's the first water of the year
It's Spring
Mani hangs a birchbark basket on the tree's skin
collecting every precious drop
there's an image on the basket

> *ÉMILIE rips a piece of birchbark on the plateforme to make a basket.*
>
> *We hear the word "mazinibaakajige" repeated several times. On the video screens the image of Thérèse Telesh Bégin from Mashteuiatsh appears. She is biting at the birchbark.*

Mazinibaakajige
Making marks on the bark
Mazinibaakajige
The art of making images on the birchbark
with your teeth

> *We hear the voice of TELESH, in French, sharing knowledge about the art of birchbark biting:*

Telesh: *It takes a lot of concentration to make images.*

> *What you imagine is what you will get.*
>
> *When I start folding, I start thinking about what I can do, what I will draw with my teeth. Most of the drawings I make, I do them in the bush, when I'm at peace, when I'm alone. That's what I've learnt.*
>
> *When Spring arrives, after Winter, that's when we feel a*

lot of energy and I always get excited because I know the bark will be beautiful.

The sap will go up and the bark will detach itself easily from the tree.

And at the same time the bark will be softer which will help to make the designs. At this point I say to people around me: don't ask me any more questions because I'm going to my forest. I'm going on a journey into the forest when I make the drawings… And by the way, it's in the way the bark is folded that you get the symmetry in the drawing... Of course, when you start to unfold, you have to be very careful because the bark is very thin.

When you look at it in the light, it will look like lace. It's exactly that.

Why do I love doing this? Because of so many generations of women before me who practiced this art form, I don't want it to disappear. They're traditions, women's traditions. I'm proud to be able to share my art. I don't want it to disappear. That's why I love to share it.

    End of the recording.

Meegwetch Telesh.
e kinamowin
acict e wabidejiin
ka ijije kendamini

    ÉMILIE gets up.

Mani
More and more I find it hard to resist your call
It sounds like the song of an old beaver

Photo by Andrée Lanthier.

SCENE 10: Rage Underwater

> *Buzzing and flashing neon lights. The rhythm*
> *changes. A sense of urgency.*

I'm in a new waiting room
a new wing of the building
I'm wearing a blue hospital gown
I'm waiting
for the voice
over the speaker
to call my name
tell me where I have to go next
the number of the cubicle where I wait some more
for him to come see me
and explain their way
of handling things.
I have an appointment with the surgeon today

Sitting on the cold table in the cubicle
I'm waiting
watching
observing
the curtains are wide open
a man comes in
collapsed in a wheelchair
they settle him in the cubicle in front of mine.
I see the translucent tube pressed into his arm
the IV hanging by his wheelchair
the tube coming out of his nose
I see his blue hospital gown
I imagine the worst
 I imagine the skeleton under the skin
I see his grey-looking skin
I see...

Menjesh Chapeney
Ants gnawing and eating from inside
Menjesh Chapeney
Abnormal cells colonizing my body

The surgeon tells me I have to take pills for the rest of my life
if I want to live

        Pause.

I have a dam in my throat.

        Blue light on the platform. ÉMILIE falls to the
        ground. Sounds of water.

I love being underwater
I love the quality of sound underwater
I love hearing my heart beat inside my ears
I hear myself better

When I was a kid
I'd love to go to the swimming pool
Every time there was a contest to see who could stay underwater
the longest
I'd win
One time
I was even able to count to 297
That's four minutes and 57 seconds
without pushing to the surface
to catch my breath
Beavers have a lot of breath too
They can stay underwater for up to fifteen minutes

        She takes a deep breath and says, in one breath:

Hold it in
until it passes
Don't take up space
Make yourself small
so small
Become invisible
Or better yet
Make others think you're invisible
Because deep down
I know
I can pretend I'm sleeping
but deep down

I know
I can't escape
It rumbles from too deep inside,
Tout finira par exploser.

> *Out of breath, ÉMILIE gasps for air.*

My mother's anger taught me how to hold my breath.

> *ÉMILIE starts to rip the birchbark on the platform, folding it with controlled gestures. The sound intensifies, each fold is like a thunderbolt.*

Take our land
Take our rights
Take our ways
Take our language
Take our wealth
Take our freedom
Take our ceremonies
Take everything

Marry a White man and you won't be buried in the soil next to your ancestors.

Decide everything for us
Who to love
How to live
Where to die
How to heal

Cut connections
Disconnect
Shut up
Repress
Hide
Build an enormous dam
Until it breaks...
Over and over again

Vulnérable
Ne pas être vulnérable

C'est pas donné à tout le monde la vulnérabilité
It's not a given
It's not for everyone
Pour survivre il faut pas que ça fonde
Surtout pas que ça fonde
Can't let your guard down
Can't get trapped
If the dam breaks
Everything will pour out
Spill out
Melt
From deep inside
And I won't be protected

Je le sais
Tu le sais
On le sait
Toutes
La vulnérabilité est un privilège
Mais pas pour nous

   Pre-recorded dialogue with VÉRONIQUE.

Véronique: «*Nowé anowé*» «*Nowé anowé*»:
    Je veux le parler. I want to speak it
    «*Nowé anowé*», *I want to speak it.*
    You have to speak it.
    Not someday. Not in the future. Now.
    «*Panema kiganowé*». *Persevere, to speak it*
    Don't give up, persevere.
    «*Sogwenden kidjamowin*».
    Give yourself the courage to speak it.

    *ÉMILIE kicks the pile of bark off the platform. Start
    of the Beaver Punk Manifesto.*

Squaw
Open your legs
So I can take your rivers
your mountains
your forest

Squaw
Open your legs

Fur trade
Skin trade
Squaw

Beaver massacre
Squaw

Cent cinquante peaux pour un fusil
Maudite sauvage

Castors exterminés
beaver
slut
Squaw

Trading pelts
for pots
guns
mirrors

Beaver hats
Ma belle Sauvage
Commerce des femmes
still today

Femme castor
Terme utilisé en France au XIXe siècle pour dire prostituée
Fucking whore

Beaver
Skinned
Scalped
Squaw

Coureurs des bois
Squaw

Coureurs de peaux
Squaw

Beavers massacred
Squaw

exterminer coloniser voler
kill rape erase
dépecer violer faire taire
steal silence displace
colonize décimer disparaître

SQUAW!

All sound stops. There is a resonating silence.

Mani weathered many storms
Mes ancêtres sont des survivantes
Moi aussi je survivrai

Photo by Andrée Lanthier.

SCENE 11: Swimming with Beavers

> *Sound of a bird flapping. Émilie stands up.*

The blue heron
Same blue as my hospital gown

It's my decision.
C'est ma décision
Nin o dedowin
Nin o dedowin
Nin o dedowin

> *Dream World starts.*
>
> *Voices come in. They encourage ÉMILIE to repeat the words after them.*
>
> *ÉMILIE gets into the canoe. As she paddles, the voices become audible like never before and give her courage to follow her inner river.*
>
> *Pre-recorded voice of Mani.*

Panema he
Panema mojik

> *ÉMILIE repeats the words live.*

Panema he
Panema mojik
Persevere
Don't give up

> *Pre-recorded voice of Mani.*

Panema oshamesh ijitigewin

> *ÉMILIE repeats the words live.*

Panema oshamesh ijitigewin
Have courage
Panema niganowé

Paddle up the river
Follow my intuition

> *Pre-recorded voice of Mani.*

Nowé anowé

> *ÉMILIE repeats the words live.*

Nowé anowé

Speak up
Always learn new words

> *Pre-recorded voice of Mani. ÉMILIE says the words at the same time.*

Kawin pededendagen
Odji madiziwin
Sogodewin

Shoapishken
Sogwenden
Sogwenden nidjamowin

> *ÉMILIE's voice only.*

Makwenden makwadizen!

> *ÉMILIE gets closer to the beavers. She disembarks from the canoe and gets on the rock. The voices fade away.*

Ni moshomik mamowi ni kokomishimik
Spend time on rocks
Ni moshomis
Spend time with elders
Visit with them
Cherish their teachings
Follow their instructions
Gather medicines
Don't take more than needed
Make offerings

Make teas
Activate medicine with a good mind

> *Pre-recorded voice of Mani. ÉMILIE says the words at the same time.*

Mishkikiwok Mitigok
N'deto Mitikok Odebi Naowa Okegendan

> *ÉMILIE's voice only.*

Decipher:
A lump in my throat
A knot on the bark
A gift in my palm

> *Call and response with beavers starts. ÉMILIE can really communicate with the beavers now.*

> *Amik arrives. Tip into Dream World. This is the third beaver dream, this time in Anishnaabemowin.*

Micha Amik!
Madage
Nadagane
Apowe
Meya makwa ejenogosijtc
Minaashin amikwan
Amik o medanan nijin
Nimenek o shkomedash
Amik ikido

> *In Amik's treated voice:*

Owé ni mashkikim
Kin oo aji
Mino abijiton

> *Excited about her progress in understanding the language, ÉMILIE translates Amik's words in English.*

This is my medicine
It's yours now
Make good use of it.

Meegwetch Amik
Odji kiguewin kidje weshbaminan

>   *Amik leaves. ÉMILIE sees them swim away this*
>   *time.*
>
>   *She puts the medicine to her throat during the*
>   *following text:*

Mitik mashkiiwin
Ka abedjiojin
Sokadeziwin
Obemenenan

>   *The voice from deep inside flows out and turns into*
>   *a song.*

Photo by Greg Hill.

SCENE 12: Inside the Lodge

> *The beams of light shining down on the platform*
> *resemble a structure made out of poles.*
>
> *ÉMILIE continues to sing, this time with words in*
> *Anishnaabemowin. She kneels on the platform while*
> *moving the beavers around her to encircle her. Her*
> *song is a prayer.*

Kitci meegwetch Kokom Mani
egijinjawotc Amik kidja weshbamok
mii e aji
e pedjimiwooga
ni Moshomisimik
ka kanidanan
tabi ke ijaik kishpen
kendanmik tebi e odjibawik.

> *Recording of Mani's voice by itself:*

Mani: *Mii e aji e pedjimiwooga ni Moshomisimik.*
        Ka kanidanan tabi
        ke ijaik kishpen kendanmik tebi e odjibawik.

> *ÉMILIE sits amongst the beavers.*

Memory of Amik is in my bones
Make good use of it
The bones of trees form dams
Making good sense of it.
The dam breaks open in my throat
Making sense of it all
Mino Abijiton
Mino Abijiton

> *ÉMILIE stands up, acknowledges everyone around*
> *her as the video projection of herself wrapped in a big*
> *piece of tent canvas appears while she's singing. In*
> *the video, she climbs on top of a beaver lodge in the*
> *middle of a pond. She exits the performance space.*

SCENE 13: Epilogue

> *The images on the copper screens change to close-ups of hands building a sweat lodge.*
>
> *Pre-recorded conversation between Émilie and Véronique comes in:*

Véronique: *Yes, it seems like a sweat lodge.* (Long pause.) *Well, there are similarities I would say because the beaver lodge it, it has a lot of trees, medicinal trees, because what the beaver, what he uses it's medicinal trees. The scent in there must be very ha... Sometimes when you just cut the trees it smells medicinal. It must be very nice and secure and the scent of the beaver...*

Émilie: *Yeah.*

Véronique: *And they're found in kind of a group also in the way they're as a big family in there. They must feeling well, healthy.*

Véronique: *Healthy in the big belly.* (Laughs.)

Émilie: *Yeah in the big belly, in the big big...beaver lodge.* (Laughs).

> *Beaver sounds intensify. Lights go off.*
>
> *There should be no applause at the end. People are invited to stay in the space and share tea. The space, theatrical until now, morphs back into installation mode like at the beginning of the performance.*
>
> *ÉMILIE comes back into the space to have tea with those who stayed.*

Photo by Andrée Lanthier.

Afterword

Lindsay Lachance

Dreams, rivers, matriarchy, beavers and birch trees. These are some key images that come to mind when I think of Émilie Monnet's *Okinum*. Many Indigenous theatre artists across Turtle Island, and particularly in what is now known as occupied Canada, use their theatre and performance practices to exercise their culturally-specific intellectual traditions, (re)learn Indigenous languages, activate political or legal systems and build dramaturgies based on material cultures like weavings, birchbark biting, traditional tattoos and other systems. This signals how Indigenous theatre practitioners are articulating and embodying theoretical understandings of life, culture, storytelling and community that are constructed differently than Western theories and worldviews. Within the field of Critical Indigenous Studies, there are growing numbers of Indigenous scholars, artists, and activists who work within Resistance and Resurgence frameworks. Resistance and Resurgence frameworks both stem from a deep love of the land, proudness of our ancestors and respect for our communities.

Through an Indigenous lens, we can understand and appreciate Émilie Monnet's play *Okinum* as a work of resurgence theory. For Michi Saagiig Nishnaabeg scholar, writer, and artist Leanne Betasamosake Simpson, kwe, meaning woman in Anishinaabemowin, is understood as resurgent method. In her chapter "Kwe as Resurgent Method," in *As We Have Always Done Indigenous Freedom Through Radical Resistance,* Simpson explains how "as political orders, [Indigenous] bodies, minds, emotions, and spirits produce theory and knowledge on a daily basis without conforming to the conventions of the academy" (31). Dreams, rivers, beavers and birch trees become the theoretical map for Monnet to question her identity, memory, and ancestral history through an interdisciplinary theatre and immersive performance experience. Amik (the beaver), came to Anishinaabe artist Émilie Monnet in her dream. A giant amik visited Monnet three times while she was fighting cancer, speaking to her in Anishinaabemowin and carrying medicine in its paw. This led Monnet to refuse Western medical cancer treatment, and she began her work with Elders, the language and the land.

Monnet exemplifies resurgence practices in her real life and her artistic practice. Her personal healing journey was devoted to learning her language, spending time at the river, learning about amik's medicines and reconciling the intergenerational trauma carried in her own body. Therefore, both formally and in terms of its content, *Okinum* resists and refuses traditional notions of Western (male) dramaturgy. Kwe as resurgent method, in this context, means that kwe is also a theorist. For Simpson, Indigenous women's bodies and life are a part of our research, and we can use this knowledge to critique and analyze.

Émilie Monnet is an actor, playwright, producer and the founder of Onishka Productions based out of Montreal, Quebec, Canada. In 2019, Onishka Productions partnered with O'Kaadenigan Wiingashk Collective to present Indigenous Contemporary Scene Scotland, a month-long program of performing arts and creative conversations featuring Indigenous artists from across Canada, presented during the Edinburgh Fringe Festival. Monnet's work as an Anishinaabe / French artist creates bridges between Indigenous and non-indigenous audiences who are mutually interested in challenging and transforming the world we live in. Monnet's work is essential in bringing Francophone and Anglophone Indigenous artistic communities together not only in Quebec, Canada, but also across the globe.

Okinum, which means dam, is a beautiful piece written in French, English and Anishinaabemowin that follows Monnet's healing journey. It is accented with a soundscape of her homelands, phrases from her language teacher and the echoes of amik chewing on some bark. Monnet uses her piece to demonstrate theatre's expansive abilities to involve characters, stage presences, and Indigenous structures that refuse the well-made play model. *Okinum* transports us between various temporal realities; the dream world, the animal plain, histories of settler-colonialisms and back to real time. Braided through *Okinum* is kwe as theory, kwe as art, kwe as survival.

A dam is a great metaphor for how Western dramatic theory and criticism does not consider Indigenous worldviews and ways of being in its pedagogy and methodology. A dam that is blocking water flow, or causing build-up, may cause more harm than good. Instead, *Okinum* is a dam that centres and celebrates Indigenous experiences, intelligences and practices.

The theoretical landscape: our rivers and trees, and the animals who make this land their home, help Indigenous theatre artists build culturally-specific dramaturgies and vessels to carry our stories. With works like Émilie Monnet's *Okinum* we see how embodied knowledge, lived experiences, land-based work and language revitalization influence both the structure and the content of a piece, building a theory of its own.

Works Cited

Simpson, Leanne Betasamosake. *As We Have Always Done: Indigenous Freedom Through Radical Resistance.* Minneapolis: University of Minnesota Press, 2017.

Lindsay Lachance's afterword is adapted from her essay "Dreaming of Rivers, Beavers and Birch Trees: Resurgence Theory in Émilie Monnet's Okinum," *which will be available in the upcoming* Routledge Anthology of Women's Theatre Theory and Dramatic Criticism, *J. Ellen Gainor and Ben Piggott, editors.*

Glossary*

Compiled by Véronique Thusky
Anishnaabe kwe from Barriere Lake, Language Consultant

[*Note: Anishnaabemowin spellings may vary.]

Amik ikido	*Amik says*
Amik o medjaminan nidjini	*Amik takes my hand*
Apawok pizagowiwok akikak	*They stand on firm earth*
Ka abedjiojin	*That they use*
Ka mashkiiwadj Mitigok	*It's the medicines in trees*
Kawin paganendaken	*Don't abandon*
Madagewok	*They swim*
Madiziwin	*Life*
Makowenden	*Remember*
Mashkwizin	*Strength*
Mashkwitagozin	*Have the strength to speak*
Mashkikiwok Mitigok	*Trees carry the medicine*
Meya Makwa ejinogosijtc	*As big as bear*
Micha Amik!	*Big beaver*
Minashini amikopea	*Beautiful shiny fur*
N'deto Mitikok Odebimen	*Listen to the Tree, their roots*
Nadagamewok	*They get close to the shore*
Nimenek mashkomedani	*Gives me a pouch*
Obamiodon	*They carry it*
Ogi mazinmidan	*Making marks on the bark*
Oshamesh ogekendanawa	*Know better*
Panema he	*That's how it is*

Panema mojik	*Always have to*
Sogodeiin	*Courage*
Sokadewin	*Strength/courage*
Showapishken	*To go through forward*

Kawin onikeken kida anishnaabemowin
Mindjamenen ki sogodewin
Ka'n acitc kidjaskanaken sagiodewin
Mii dac ke mossekidamen kida ijitcigeiin
Kishpen nisistemin anishnaabemowin
Ningan wasek kiga ijionagon.

> *Do not forget Anishnaabemowin*
> *Your language*
> *Cultivate the spirit of courage*
> *Preserve the love in you*
> *It will strengthen your heart and spirit.*
> *The language will integrate itself in all that you do*
> *And it will take you far into the future.*

Kawin ni potosin, nida animowe gotc

> *I persevere, I speak it*

Nid-nimakowag
Ni moshomik mamowi ni kokomik
Meegwetc nidanak eki pakidanajiwodj kidji weshibadiman amik mashkikimin
Kijedjigewin mamowi kigewin atsokan owe
Apidendagozi aa Micha Amik kagi bi ijitcigetc

> *I acknowledge my ancestors*
> *I give thanks to my dream of beaver and for their medicine*
> *The story of Creation is a story that can heal*
> *Beaver has a special role in the Creation story*

Ohska Madiziwin mojak madjitamigan
Kiga pakidedan panema kidja togok madiziiwin
Kek oshka madiziwin kida ane togok

> *Life is a constant birth*
> *Sacrifice brings new life*
> *One life is given up for another to begin*

Owe ni mashkikim
Kin oo aji
Mino abijadton

> *This is my medicine*
> *This medicine is yours now*
> *Make good use of it*

Meegwetch, Telesh
Egi kakinamojiin
Acict e wabidejiin
Ka ija kendamini

> *Thank you Telesh*
> *For your teaching*
> *And to have shown me*
> *Your knowledge*

Okinum Podcast Series

In conjunction with the National Arts Centre production of Okinum in the fall of 2021, Émilie conducted some interviews for a special podcast series created in collaboration with la Scène Nationale du Son and Transistor Media. Transcripts of two of the podcast episodes follow.

Interview with Simon Brascoupé

Stories of giant beavers continue to be told today.

Émilie:

In this episode I speak with Simon Brascoupé, Algonquin-Mohawk artist from Kitigan Zibi, now living in Ottawa. Simon shares the story of the giant beaver that I first heard when we met up in Scotland. We discussed the importance of knowing the land we live on and the stories that forged it.

Simon:

When I tell that story—and I tell it across Canada—and other people have giant beaver stories and giant animal stories that really go back. You know, this giant beaver that dams up that area that has the highest tides in the world... So the beaver decides to dam up this waterway to capture a whale. And the whale realizes it's trapped in this dam and it flaps its tail and the water breaks the dam and the water goes out and it comes back in and it goes out...and that's why they say the tide is so high there [Bay of Fundy]. It's an old Algonquin story that's been documented; being an academic, I checked it out. There's quite a number of references in the literature about this particular story and what's beautiful about it is that it's situated in Algonquin territory.

So if you can imagine this giant beaver, about 600 pounds, as big as a bear, roaming around this territory. And Wesakejak, the trickster, decides one day that he wants to eat this giant beaver. So he goes up the Kichi Sibi, what's now known as the Ottawa River, and he goes north into Quebec near the Lac Dumoine area and there's this big beaver in the river and he's got his lodge in the water. So he decides that even though he's a really good swimmer, he decides to lower the water. So he breaks the beaver's dam and the water starts running out. But Wesakejak is also kind of lazy, you know, and he's tired after breaking the dam and falls asleep. So of course when he wakes up, the beaver's gone. And he gets kind of upset. But he follows the beaver's tracks south and gets near the upper end of the Ottawa River and he spots another dam. But this time he brings a buddy with him and he told his buddy, "I want you to keep an eye on that beaver, because last time he snuck away on me." So he starts to dig up the dam, breaks up the dam, and the water's running out. And Wesakejak falls asleep. And his buddy tries to wake him up, he's shaking him, shaking him. Doesn't wake him up. And by the time he wakes up, of course the beaver's gone again. And Wesakejak gets so mad that he kicks his buddy. And he kicks him straight up into the sky and he goes up so high that he turns into a rock. And then he lands on the Algonquin territory.

And if you walk anywhere in Algonquin territory, even in the city of Ottawa where I live, you know, you see rocks everywhere. My kids used to ask my dad, "Where did all these rocks come from?" And he says, "Oh, one day it just rained all these rocks."

So Wesakejak doesn't give up and he goes east on the Ottawa River, down around Calumet Island. So, Calumet Island was a place historically where Algonquins would go and settle feuds and fights and all those sorts of things. Calumet Island is still an important island for Algonquins. But there's chutes there. So the giant beaver builds a dam and Wesakejak breaks it, but both Wesakejak and the beaver are getting old so the old beaver goes a little bit north off the river and dies. And he forms these, like, hills. So when you look at the hills on the Ottawa River, they all look like these giant beavers. And you can see Wesakejak's little tracks on the riverbanks in the rock near the chute.

Today we kind of analyze everything... So beavers are these bio-engineers: they've created the land. So after the glaciers have melted heading north, they created all these waterways and streams and then the beaver starts damming them up. But you can imagine in thousands of years, these little dams become bigger dams, they become lakes. So the beaver really created the territory that we live in, where we all inhabit. So it's a good way to think about the land, how it was formed, that it took thousands of years. The giant beavers and the beavers as we know them today contributed to the making of the territory.

The beaver plays a really important role in our history, but I think this whole business of when our spirit comes into the world, when we're born, that spirit already knows everything. It's parents' job, grandparents' job to remind that spirit of things it should know. But that spirit, our learning spirit, also learns from animals. I'm from the Bear clan, so I get inspired by a lot of things by bear, but also I can learn from beavers, I can learn from otters… They are there to teach us. So the land becomes our teacher. And we learn how to live off the land, we learn how to live sustainably off the land. You know, I think we talked before about the beaver almost becoming extinct, and the beaver's coming back; the beaver's telling us something. You know, that maybe we're doing something right. Yeah. So it's out there to give us a message.

Émilie:
In the grandfathers' and grandmothers' teachings about the seven values, Beaver represents wisdom. Why do you think the beaver is so wise? Or why did we allocate that value to Amik?

Simon:
I've never really thought about it, but you know, what is wisdom? Wisdom is something that we gain through our lives. Of course, we're probably wise as children. But as we grow up, we become less wise and then we become wiser. And if you look at the beaver, and all the stories we just were reminiscing about, the beaver is telling us… The beaver must have had an impact not only on Indigenous Peoples but Europeans in that the beaver is industrious. It's working hard, you know, it's working all the time. It's building something… A lot of people look at animals as not having the same intelligence as humans, but I think we overrate ourselves. You know, we're destroying the world—I don't think that's wise. The beaver is wise because it's demonstrating to us that we work hard, we live with the natural world with the tools that we have. The beaver is telling that we need to prepare for the future; they build the dam, it's thinking about the future in many ways, the generations that come.

All we have to do is just look at the beaver, you know, as far as many things... I did an art project over the last four or five years; we were making a paddle installation for Pimisi Station. I heard this story many times: people would say that Algonquins historically didn't have a canoe, and one day somebody was skinning a beaver and they opened up a beaver's chest and there were all these ribs. Of course, we know the beaver is an amazing swimmer, so it inspired the birchbark canoe. And then you look at the tail; the tail is the beavertail paddle. So you can see where the wisdom comes in. How wise is the beaver to teach us how to live sustainably not only on the land but on the water?

Émilie:
The beaver is a very generous creature. It's gifting us with knowledge. It's like we have to be more attentive, or pay more attention to everything around us, because all the answers are there.

Simon:
Yeah. And particularly with COVID. It's really slowed me down... I'm the kind of person that's always busy, you know? And sometimes I don't pay enough attention to what's around me. Like the little details. Like how to fix something. I try to fix something. and I break it. But now I'm fixing it and I'm actually fixing it. Mother Earth is telling us something.

Interview with Floyd Favel

Stories can heal. Amik is my kin.

Émilie:

In this episode, I speak with Cree playwright and theatre director Floyd Favel from Poundmaker, Saskatchewan. This is a conversation on the medicine of stories, and the reciprocity in the relationship between animals and humans.

Floyd:

When we speak of Indigenous theatre, it goes beyond style, method, form. It is about the unconscious. But "unconscious" is a Jungian term, it's a western European term. What we say is, "Spirit World." Spirits, in Cree "acahk" means a spirit. With our tradition, any animal, any being can enter your ceremony and they will use the voice of the "shaman," a sort of medium. They will use his voice, his vocal cords, and they will speak through him or her. I've seen those ceremonies when I was young and they're still around, and there's still people who can do that. But in my case, not as a ceremony but as a creative act, the beaver he told me the story that I wrote. He spoke through me and I wrote it down. And very often, sometimes as Indigenous artists we exaggerate or mythologize an experience just to create a fiction, because theatre is a fiction. And sometimes in our life, we create a fiction. But in this case, there is no fiction. Very often I think of other Indigenous playwrights and I admire them, how they are able to write so many plays. Some of them just sit down and write a play and go to a dramaturg and get it worked on. But any play I wrote always came in a rhythm, in a burst of energy in one or two days or four days. In this case it was four days, when I wrote about this beaver.

Émilie:

Like a ceremony.

Floyd:

Yes, I was visiting… It was shortly after my mother whose "smile brightened the world," had departed for the Spirit World. I had gone to Washington, DC and New York during which I had felt it coming on, the story…something coming on, but I didn't know what. Often in the middle of the day, no matter where I was, if I was in a park or a restaurant, I would almost fall asleep. I would need to be in a dark quiet for a couple hours. I left these cities and I went to visit a friend in Vermont. I arrived, I said hello, and I went to my room in the attic. And I basically stayed there for four or five days. I would come down once in a while and there would be a plate of food for me and I would eat it and then I would make some coffee and I would go back up.

It was in that time I would hear a rhythm in my mind or in my spirit, and the first thing I heard was "Hau nosim!" That was the first thing I heard which was, "Hey, Grandson! I wanna tell you something." And then I would listen and he said, "Peyakow mena." which is "Once upon a time." It continued and said in Cree, "I was good-looking once, but to look at me, you would not think that I had been good-looking." And so I started to write. And then I would add, create, and then when I would get lost, I would hear a voice again, carrying me forward. So that voice, that rhythm, those sentences in Cree… Like little threads of sentences, would carry me along until the next step of the story. So it was half me, and half this voice. But at that time, I was more young and not so knowledgeable. But nowadays, from what I've heard from spiritual leaders, elders, they always say: "When you work with the spiritual dimension, half of it is you, and the other half is the other side. You have to do half the work." At that time I found that to be true. Because I wasn't passively listening and passively writing, like automatic writing, I was working with it, reaching it, working for it. Sometimes I'd feel I'd lost it and then I would kind of backtrack in the story and I'd find the right place again and keep going and then I'd hear another voice, another progression. Sometimes I would fall to the floor and weep.

So I guess if there is somebody who had taught me Indigenous theatre, nobody ever taught me that me what I was experiencing, but I had heard stories by listening to old people. Telling stories about animals. That was my study, you could say. And then it came time that something dramatic happened in my life, like the death of my mother. And from there it emerged that then the spirit being could tell me a story, I guess to heal me and to help me. Because the story that I eventually wrote was the Beaver and the death of all his relatives, and his grief and his mourning. So in a way, what white people call metaphor or analogy, that's what it was. But with Indigenous people we don't say that, we say "ay atayukat," he told a sacred story. In in that sacred story, in "atayukawin," he healed you. It was beyond metaphor, beyond analogy, and beyond simile, and it simply became a healing story—but within the realm of theatre. Because it was told to me in a series of voices like a dramatic monologue. So it went beyond theatre, almost into like a super-theatre, or a para-theatre. A para-theatre that went on the fringes of theatre and I guess the borders of cultural theory, the borders of storytelling, and it goes deep into the unconscious and you're roaming in that field, you're roaming in that dialogue and you're in a very fragile state. So because you're dealing with an actual death, an actual grief, it's affecting your energy, your body and then voila—you hear a story! And was that story. And that's how it came to me and that's what that story was.

To this day I always remember it. If somebody was to ask me, Floyd, tell me your process of being a playwright, I would say I'm not a playwright, I'm not a dramatist. I would say I probably sincerely only wrote one drama, and that was *Master of the Dew*. That was a true process. That was the one process we always seek, that I sought in my theatre training in Europe and in different places around the world.

Émilie:
You're saying that you're hearing a voice at first. When did you figure out it was the voice of the beaver?

Floyd:
Through the story. Through the story that the being was telling me. That he had been good-looking; he had been swimming along the creeks, living in his lodge. And in his lodge, the roof of his

lodge was the sky. Just like us, we have a sky. But what we see when we see a beaver, is we see a lodge and we just think it's a bunch of mud and dirt. But for them it's a sky, just like we have a sky. And then the walls, we just think it's mud and dirt, but for them it's a horizon, too. And they have a little mound of earth in there. We think it's a pile of mud, but for them it's an earth. It's kind of like a micro-world like our macro-world. So that's what...the beaver was telling me that's how their world was. He said he was a beaver, so I could only assume he was a beaver.

Émilie:
And what did he teach you? What did you learn from him, from that experience?

Floyd:
I guess his greatest teaching for me was: Transform your experiences into art, into something that can be shared. You know, when you start to think of Indigenous people and their relationship, I guess their connection to nature... We talk about connection to nature, well that's that. That's working with them. Paying them. So it's like, reciprocal. You must always work with them, give back what they give you. All spiritual beings, all animals they voluntarily give their lives to us, to sustain us. That's their pact. That's what they told the Great Spirit. They voluntarily did that. So then once we start looking at them as a commodity, then yeah, I think we have broken a spiritual law.

The only thing you can go on is your dreams. Those are like your thread, Ariadne's thread. So you must follow that. And they're not formulas; they're not A to B to C. It's not like school, they're very different from a western education. And because this Indigenous education that follows dreams, it's a total education, you must be immersed in it. And then you must live it, minute by minute. One of the main factors in dreams and spiritual knowledge is that they say you're always being watched. Even by animals, like a beaver from a creek.

Photo by Clark Ferguson.